JACK HORNER,
DINOSAUR HUNTER!

Written by
SOPHIA GHOLZ

Illustrated by
DAVE SHEPHARD

CRUNCH. SWOOSH.

As a baby, Jack's lullaby was the sound of his father's gravel trucks digging in Montana.

And as soon he was able, Jack dug along with them.

He was a boy who thrived outdoors, among trees, dirt—and dinosaurs.

Jack understood dinosaurs weren't alive anymore, but he wished they were.

He dreamed of becoming a paleontologist—hunting for dinosaur bones in the ground. But Jack only found . . .

sticks,

dirt,

and gravel.

Until one day . . .

he spied a peculiar rock.
Jack swept the sand aside.

CRUNCH. SWOOSH.

CRUNCH. SWOOSH.
A clamshell!

He looked across his small backyard and pictured an ocean covering the land millions of years ago—an ocean filled with ancient beasts. This wasn't a dinosaur bone, but it was his first fossil. Jack wanted more.

He trained his eyes to search for clues among the rocks: irregular textures, colors, and shapes. Soon, he had a whole collection of fossilized shells. But Jack's heart longed most for dinosaurs.

He begged his parents to take him fossil hunting . . .

around town,

in the woods,

near the mountains.

One summer day, while hiking a crop of cliffs, Jack spied an odd rock nestled in the ground. Sweat dripping, heart racing, he leapt into action.

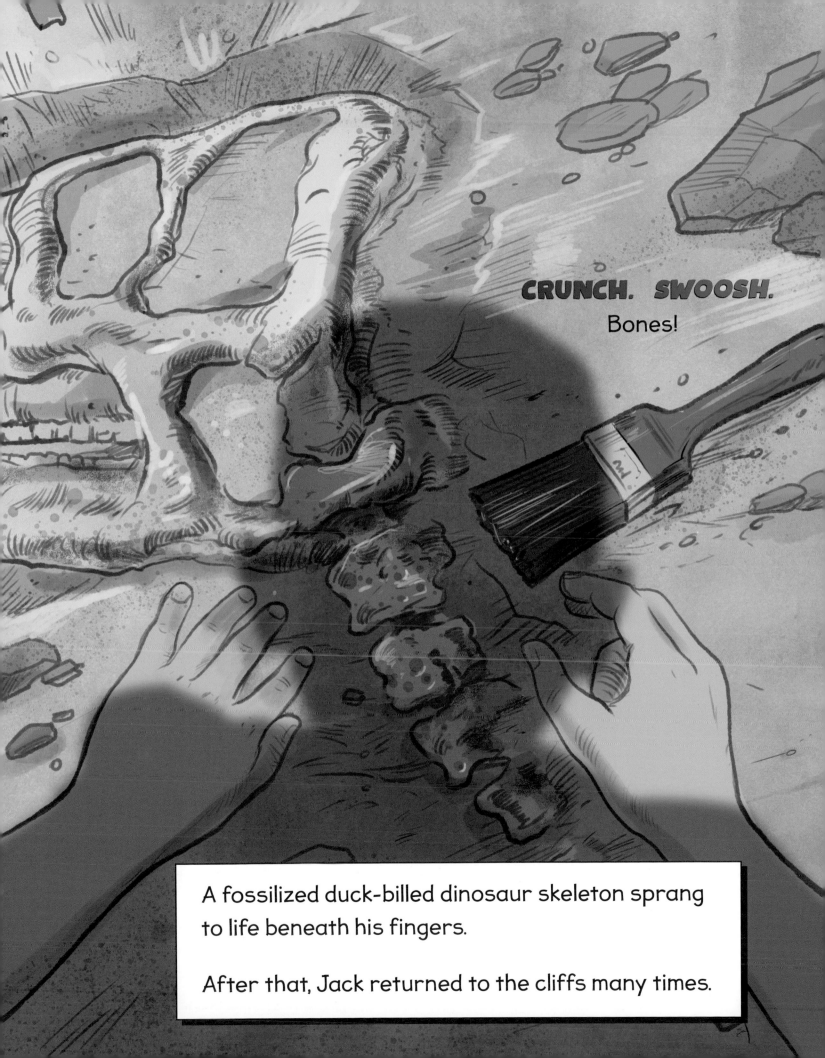

CRUNCH. SWOOSH.

Bones!

A fossilized duck-billed dinosaur skeleton sprang to life beneath his fingers.

After that, Jack returned to the cliffs many times.

Outdoors, he was becoming a fossil expert.
Indoors, Jack struggled with school.

He could easily read the lines of a landscape—
finding places fossils lay hidden—or the edges of
bones like pieces to a puzzle. But where most kids
saw words and equations, Jack saw a jumble of
letters and numbers that didn't make sense.

His teachers warned that if Jack couldn't pass his classes, he'd never become a paleontologist. Struggling to read, his grades dropped. But he wouldn't give up. Instead, Jack decided to learn as much about science as he could on his own.

In the basement of his house, Jack experimented.

His Tesla coil *sizzled* and *popped*.

A Van de Graaff generator made his hair stand straight up.

A crowd gathered to watch his homemade rocket launch thousands of feet into the sky. Jack failed his classes, but his science projects won awards.

One project was so impressive it caught the attention of a prestigious university. Finally, with fossils on his mind, Jack left for college—ready to become a paleontologist.

But his dreams quickly crumbled.

Still struggling to read, Jack failed his classes and had to drop out of school before he finished his first year.

Not long after, he received a letter drafting him into the United States military. Before he knew it, Jack said goodbye to Montana and flew across the world to join the Vietnam War.

But even in war, his heart roamed with the dinosaurs. Jack made a decision: if he couldn't be a paleontologist himself, he wanted to work as close to them as possible.

When he returned home, Jack sent letters to museums searching for a job. It was Princeton University's natural history museum that answered, and Jack was thrilled to accept their offer.

At the museum, Jack assembled and cataloged exhibits, working closely with the scientists. His colleagues discovered that, although he had a hard time reading words, Jack was an expert at reading fossils.

Before long, he received a promotion and . . .

One summer day, as the team hiked a crop of cliffs, Jack spied something odd. Heart thumping like the tail of an *Ankylosaurus*, he leapt into action.

An egg formed beneath his fingers—but not just any egg. This was a fully intact, fossilized dinosaur embryo—one of the first found in the world.

After that, Jack and the team returned to the cliffs many times.

They excavated entire sites filled with fossilized eggs, proving dinosaurs nested in colonies.

Jack named a new dinosaur species—the *Maiasaura*!

He became a specialist on dinosaur behavior and argued that some dinosaurs were more like birds than ferocious reptiles. He claimed dinosaurs were social and cared for their babies—like humans!

Jack had always seen things differently. Now his research helped the world see things differently too.

Years later, when Hollywood producers needed a dinosaur specialist on the set of a blockbuster movie, they called the person who had inspired the main character...

. . . world-famous paleontologist, expert dinosaur hunter Jack Horner.

CRUNCH. SWOOSH.

Jack understands dinosaurs aren't alive anymore,

but he wishes they were.

AUTHOR'S NOTE

While researching another topic, I came across quotes from Jack Horner that piqued my interest. I continued to research, this time focusing on Jack. In a textbook world, here was a person who had mostly forged his own path. Jack suffered from a reading disorder. But what sets us apart does not have to hold us back, it just means we have to dig a little differently. Despite his struggles, Jack never stopped dreaming of paleontology. What do you dream of?

MORE ABOUT JACK HORNER

John "Jack" Horner was born in Shelby, Montana, in 1946. For the first few months of his life, he shared a tent with his family (and a bull snake) by the Marias River, where Jack's dad operated a gravel business. As a child, Jack's parents encouraged his love of dinosaurs and fossil hunting, often taking him to explore the national parks around them. It was on one of those trips that he found his first dinosaur bone, at age eight, and later his first dinosaur skeleton at age thirteen. These finds fueled Jack's dreams of becoming a paleontologist.

Despite his love of learning, Jack struggled in school due to severe and undiagnosed dyslexia. He made many attempts at college, but never successfully graduated or received a college degree. Still, he forged ahead. In 1975, Jack caught a break when he landed a job as a technician at Princeton University's natural history museum. While at Princeton, Jack was officially diagnosed with dyslexia. Though he still couldn't read well, the diagnosis helped him understand his struggles and better work around them. Recognizing his hard work, Jack was eventually promoted to research assistant

and, after that, he took the lead on research projects of his own.

In 1978, while performing fieldwork in Montana, Jack and his colleagues unearthed the nesting site of fifteen baby duck-billed dinosaurs. These were the first egg clutches found in North America and provided evidence that dinosaurs nested in colonies. Through this find, Jack proved that dinosaurs cared for their young—a discovery that changed the way people perceive dinosaurs altogether. Over the next few decades, Jack named new dinosaur species and showed the world that dinosaurs may have more in common with birds than reptiles.

Jack Horner became one of the leading paleontologists of our time. Today, he continues to work in the field and push the boundaries of how the world views dinosaurs. If you've watched a Jurassic Park movie, you might be familiar with Jack. He not only served as a dinosaur consultant on all of the films, he also inspired one of the main characters.

DINO LAB

Imagine you are out in the field searching for fossils, and you discover the skeleton of a never-before-seen dinosaur.

Design your dinosaur: Draw a picture of the type of dinosaur you found. Is it tall or short? Does it walk on two legs or four legs? Perhaps it has a long neck or almost no neck at all. Does it have a tail, claws, spikes, or beautiful feathered wings? Have fun with your design.

Name your dinosaur: Scientists name dinosaurs after many things. Sometimes the name will describe something interesting about the dinosaur. For example, a *Triceratops* is named for the three (tri) horns on its head. Dinosaurs are also named after the places they are found, the way they behaved, or even the person who discovered them. Look at the Greek and Latin words below and see if you can pair them together to describe your brand-new dinosaur. Or make up a new name of your own.

Acu — sharp	**Fort** — strong	**Saur, Saurus** — lizard
Bi — two	**Magna** — large	**Scler** — hard
Canthas — spiked	**Mega** — great	**Tri** — three
Celer — fast	**Micro** — small	**Urus** — tail
Ceros — horned	**Mono** — one	**Xeno** — weird
Compso — pretty	**Ornitho** — bird	
Derm — skin	**Ortho** — straight	
Dino — terrible	**Ped** — foot	
Dont — tooth		

For everyone out there who has had to learn to dig a little differently,
and for Jeff who never gives up.

— Sophia

Thank you to my two boys, Albie and Japhy,
for digging in the dirt while I sketched.

— Dave

SLEEPING BEAR PRESS™

2395 South Huron Parkway, Suite 200
Ann Arbor, MI 48104
www.sleepingbearpress.com

Printed and bound in the United States.

10 9 8 7 6 5 4 3 2 1

Library of Congress Cataloging-in-Publication Data

Names: Gholz, Sophia M., author. | Shephard, David (Illustrator), illustrator.
Title: Jack Horner : dinosaur hunter / by Sophia Gholz ; illustrated by Dave Shephard.
Description: Ann Arbor, Michigan : Sleeping Bear Press, [2021] | Audience: Ages 6-10 |
Summary: "When Jack Horner was a child, he was fascinated by dinosaur fossils.
He hunted for them and dreamed of being a great paleontologist. But Jack struggled
with school and reading. Jack found his own way to success and became one of the
world's most famous paleontologist!"— Provided by publisher.
Identifiers: LCCN 2021010658 | ISBN 9781534111196 (hardcover)
Subjects: LCSH: Horner, John R.—Juvenile literature. |
Paleontologists—United States—Biography—Juvenile literature.
Classification: LCC QE707.H67 G46 2021 | DDC 567.9092 [B]—dc23
LC record available at https://lccn.loc.gov/2021010658